MW01716466

RAISED WITH CHRIST

A HOLY WEEK STUDY

WILL BURROWS

Raised With Christ

Published by Hosanna Revival
4 Kovach Dr, Suite 430
Cincinnati, OH 45215

Cover design: Hosanna Revival

Cover photo: "L'Ascension" by Gustave Doré, 1879. Public Domain.

First printing 2023

All emphases in Scripture quotations have been added by the author.

Paperback ISBN: 978-1-954053-22-9

IF THEN YOU HAVE BEEN RAISED WITH CHRIST, SEEK THE THINGS THAT ARE ABOVE, WHERE CHRIST IS, SEATED AT THE RIGHT HAND OF GOD. SET YOUR MINDS ON THINGS THAT ARE ABOVE, NOT ON THINGS THAT ARE ON EARTH. FOR YOU HAVE DIED, AND YOUR LIFE IS HIDDEN WITH CHRIST IN GOD. WHEN CHRIST WHO IS YOUR LIFE APPEARS, THEN YOU ALSO WILL APPEAR WITH HIM IN GLORY.

Colossians 3:1-4

TABLE OF CONTENTS

INTRODUCTION

Dutch theologian and pastor Anthony Hoekema (1913-1988) once wrote, "Once you have your eyes opened to this concept of union with Christ, you will find it almost everywhere in the New Testament."[1] In my experience, he is absolutely right. The more I studied this concept, the more it leapt off the pages of Scripture—I couldn't "unsee" it.

The New Testament describes the Christian's union with Christ in two ways:

1. We are in Christ
   John 15:4-5, 7; 1 Corinthians 15:22; 2 Corinthians 5:17, 12:2; Galatians 3:28; Ephesians 1:4, 2:10; Philippians 3:9; 1 Thessalonians 4:16; 1 John 4:13

2. Christ is in us
   Romans 8:10; 2 Corinthians 13:5; Galatians 2:20; Ephesians 3:17; Colossians 1:27[2]

---

1 Anthony Hoekema, *Saved By Grace* (Grand Rapids, MI: Eerdmans Publishing, 1989), 64.

2 Hoekema's quotes cited by Justin Taylor, "Union With Christ: A Crash Course," February 10, 2011, *Between Two Worlds*, https://www.thegospelcoalition.org/blogs/justin-taylor/union-with-christ-a-crash-course/, accessed May 5, 2022.

Union with Christ is a work of the Triune God. It was planned by the Father, Son, and Holy Spirit in eternity past (Ephesians 1:3-14). Therefore, our union with Christ is rooted in God's divine plan to save sinners. The basis of our union with Christ is his redemptive work for us, namely his death, burial, and resurrection. Finally, *actual* union with Christ is established with us in time. In other words, though this plan was set in motion before time began, it became an actual reality within the framework of space and time. Jesus Christ—who existed in eternity past with the Father and Holy Spirit, unbound by space or time—entered our world as a flesh-and-blood man to make this glorious plan a reality.

The very God of the universe had to enter our broken world to accomplish this great plan. My hope for this short study is for us to meditate on our union with Christ together using Hoekema's outline as a guide to help us understand that the whole of our salvation—from beginning to end—is *in Christ*. There may be some unfamiliar words in the following outline, but I will do my best to explain these important terms as they come up.

OUTLINE

1. We are initially united to Christ in *regeneration.*
   Ephesians 2:4-5, 10

2. We appropriate and continue to live out of this union through *faith.*
   Galatians 2:20; Ephesians 3:16-17

3. We are *justified* in union with Christ.
   2 Corinthians 5:21; Philippians 3:8-9

4. We are *sanctified* through union with Christ.
   1 Corinthians 1:30; John 15:4-5; 2 Corinthians 5:17

5. We *persevere* in the life of faith in union with Christ.
   John 10:27-29; Romans 8:38-39; Jude 24-25

6. We are even said to *die* in Christ.
   Galatians 2:20; Romans 6:6-14, 14:8; 1 Thessalonians 4:16; Revelation 14:13

7. We shall be *raised* with Christ.
   Colossians 3:1; 1 Corinthians 15:22

8. We shall be eternally *glorified* with Christ.
   Colossians 3:4; 1 Thessalonians 4:16-17

We will meditate on these eight points of our union with Christ over the next eight days. Scottish theologian and Presbyterian minister Sinclair Ferguson noted that "if we are united to Christ, then we are united to him in all points of his activity on our behalf." In other words, we cannot be united to Christ in his resurrection if we are not united to Christ in his death—we are either united to Christ or we are not. Ferguson continued this thought by saying that union with Christ "is rooted not in humanity and their achievement of holiness or sanctification, but in what God has done in Christ, and for us in union with him."[3]

This is a glorious truth—Christ has done it all! No amount of human striving could ever amount to a single moment of union with Christ, but God has—in Christ—done the work of reconciling us to himself, initiating this glorious union.

It is my prayer and desire that this study will cause you to marvel at what God has done for you in Christ to unite you to himself for all eternity.

Soli Deo Gloria!

---

3 Sinclair Ferguson, *Christian Spirituality: Five Views of Sanctification* (Downers Grove, IL: IVP Academic, 1989), 58.

HOW TO USE THIS DEVOTIONAL

Each day will consist of three parts: Read, Meditate, and Coram Deo.

READ

The Word of God is alive, powerful, and capable of discerning the thoughts and intentions of your heart (Hebrews 4:12). It is profitable for every believer because every word of it has been inspired by God himself (2 Timothy 3:16). Therefore, each day will begin with a passage of Scripture. I don't want to make statements of my own, then patch Scripture together to support my claims. Rather, I want to open the Word first and draw out what it is saying to us. Ultimately, my words are not worth all that much, but if they can point you to the Word of God, then I will have accomplished what I set out to do.

MEDITATE

Reading the Bible is something every Christian should do—the words of God are our very life (Deuteronomy 32:47). However, we're a fast-paced people. It's too easy to skim a passage of Scripture, shut the book, and carry on with the rest of our day. Joshua commanded God's people in Joshua 1:8 to meditate on the Book of the Law day and night. This was their Bible—the words of God Moses had written down. The psalmist picks this idea up in the very first psalm: "But his delight is in the law of the LORD, and on his law he meditates day and night" (Psalm 1:2). Each day will include prompts and questions to help you reflect on the Scripture you've just read so you can store it up in your heart (Psalm 119:11).

CORAM DEO

Coram Deo is a Latin phrase that refers to something that takes place in the presence of, or before the face of, God. "To live *coram Deo* is to live one's entire life in the presence of God, under the authority of God, to the glory of God."[1] As we read and meditate on the Word of God, we are conformed to the image of Christ by the power of his Word and Spirit. Each day will end with a *coram Deo* thought that seeks to answer the following question: How am I to live in light of what I have just read in God's Word, knowing that I am living *coram Deo* (before the face of God)? James tells us we ought not be people who simply hear the Word of God, but don't "do" it (James 1:22). Through his Word and Spirit, God renews our minds, bringing about *real* life change. Live life before the face of God and for his glory.

Let's begin!

1 R. C. Sproul, "What Does 'Coram Deo' Mean?" *Ligonier.org*, November 13, 2017, https://www.ligonier.org/learn/articles/what-does-coram-deo-mean.

MADE ALIVE IN CHRIST

Day 1

READ: EPHESIANS 2:1-10

From the outside, the events of Holy Week seem like a grand plan gone horribly wrong. Jesus enters Jerusalem to excited cheers and shouts of "Hosanna to the Son of David! Blessed is he who comes in the name of the Lord! Hosanna in the highest!" (Matthew 21:9). Their cry reveals something of their knowledge of messianic prophecy: They knew a Messiah would come from the house and line of David.[1] And here he was, entering their city like a king! By Friday, Jesus would be hanging dead on a cross.

Later, after Jesus had risen and ascended into heaven, the apostle Peter was preaching a powerful message about the cross—and what *really* happened during Holy Week.

---

1 The people are quoting from Psalm 118:25. They are literally crying out, "Save us! Save us!"

> "Men of Israel, hear these words: Jesus of Nazareth, a man attested to you by God with mighty works and wonders and signs that God did through him in your midst, as you yourselves know—this Jesus, delivered up according to the definite plan and foreknowledge of God, you crucified and killed by the hands of lawless men."
> *Acts 2:22-23*

Peter makes an astounding claim here. He recognizes that the crowd to whom he is speaking is responsible for the death of Christ ("This Jesus...you crucified and killed"), and yet, he says Jesus was delivered up to this crucifixion and killing "according to the definite plan and foreknowledge of God." This was no grand plan gone wrong—everything happened exactly as it had been planned in eternity past by the Father, Son, and Holy Spirit (Ephesians 1:3-14). Jesus walked willingly and knowingly to the cross to lay down his life. But *why*? Scripture reveals many answers to that question—all of them true and complementary. The one answer I want to consider today is this: to make you *alive*.

Martin Luther used the phrase "the wonderful exchange" to describe what happened on the cross. Our sin was laid on Christ—the perfect, spotless Lamb of God—and his righteousness was applied to all who would trust in him alone for salvation. The godly died in the place of the ungodly (Romans 5:6). The righteous died in the place of the unrighteous (1 Peter 3:18). In laying down his life, Jesus completed the work he was sent to do—that is why he cried "It is finished" when he died (John 19:30). He was not acting alone and his plan did not fail; he was carrying out the plan of redemption set forth by the Triune God in eternity past—before the foundations of the earth were laid.

> "He chose us in him before the foundation of the world, that we should be holy and blameless before him."
> *Ephesians 1:4*

When we consider Ephesians 1:4, namely that God has chosen us to be holy and blameless, a problem comes to light: *we are not holy and blameless*. We are nothing like God. In his letter to the Romans, Paul cites the Psalms to describe our state: "None is righteous, no, not one; no one understands; no one seeks for God. All have turned aside; together they have become worthless; no one does good, not even one" (Romans 3:10-12).[2] Once again, it would seem as though God's grand plan has gone awry. Have God's promises failed? Not at all. Ephesians 2:1 brings some much needed clarity: "You were *dead*."

When I was a kid, salvation was sometimes explained using a picture of a drowning man bobbing to and fro in the tempestuous waves of an angry sea. Another man would come along in a dingy and throw a lifesaver to the drowning man and save him just before he drowns. The example is simple enough: the drowning man is a person without Christ, and the man in the dingy is a Christian who rescues the drowning man with the saving message of the gospel. Some images would have Jesus throwing

2 Cited from Psalm 14:1-3 and Psalm 53:1-3.

a lifesaver, but the point remains the same: Jesus is the only way to be saved. However, this example has a major problem when compared to Scripture: any person at risk of drowning in a stormy sea is doing everything they can to stay afloat. They are kicking their legs, moving their arms, regulating their breathing, and screaming at the top of their lungs, hoping someone will hear and come to their rescue.

Paul paints a very different picture. To stick with the ocean metaphor, Paul would say we are not fighting for life in an angry sea—we're at the bottom of the ocean, lying dead in a watery grave. No movement, no seeking help, no crying for salvation. *We are dead.*

This strong choice of words helps us understand the reality of our lives before Christ. Of course, we were living, breathing people, but we were dead to Christ. We didn't know God and we didn't care to know God. We weren't seeking after him. We were slaves to self and Satan. "But God, being rich in mercy, because of the great love with which he loved us, even when we were dead in our trespasses, *made us alive* together with Christ" (Ephesians 2:4-5, emphasis mine). The apostle Paul wrote in his letter to Titus,"when the goodness and loving kindness of God our Savior appeared, *he saved us*, not because of works done by us in righteousness, but according to his own mercy, by the washing of regeneration and renewal of the Holy Spirit, whom he poured out on us richly through Jesus Christ our Savior, so that being justified by his grace we might become heirs according to the hope of eternal life" (Titus 3:4-7, emphasis mine).

Being made alive together with Christ—being regenerated—begins a brand new life with Christ! This is why Jesus calls it being "born again" (John 3:3). Paul is quite intentional with his word choice in Ephesians 2 and Titus 3. You were *dead.* God made you *alive. He* saved *you.*

We are not merely sick people whom Christ can make better. We are not merely bad people whom Christ can make "good." Apart from Christ, we are *dead* in our trespasses and sins, and in Christ, God makes us *alive.* We are regenerated by his power alone, according to his gracious mercy. Only the power of God could do such a thing! The power that raised Christ from the dead is the same power that says to us while we are dead in our sins: "Live!" When God makes us alive, we are moved from death into a new life with a new purpose, new desires, and a new heart (Ezekiel 36:26; Psalm 37:4).

If you have been united to Christ, you have been made alive in Christ! Read back over the first three verses of Ephesians 2. Note the word "were." You *were* dead in your trespasses and sins. You *were* a slave to self and Satan. You *were* living under the wrath of God. No longer! Paul writes in Romans 8:1, "There is therefore now no condemnation for those who are in Christ Jesus." He writes a few verses later, "If the Spirit of him who raised Jesus from the dead dwells in you, he who raised Christ Jesus from the dead will also give life to your mortal bodies through his Spirit who dwells in you" (Romans 8:11). God has made you alive! Walk in that newness of life (Romans 6:4).

MEDITATE

Apart from regeneration, we cannot stand before God—and we certainly could never hope to be made alive outside of Christ. If you are in Christ, meditate on what it means for you to be made alive in Christ today. Consider Jesus Christ, who became sin for you, so that in him, you might become the righteousness of God (2 Corinthians 5:21). Your life came through his death.

CORAM DEO

In Ephesians 2:1-3, Paul describes the life of a person before they meet Christ. In verses 4-9, he details the work God has done for us in Christ. In verse 10, he reveals one of the reasons God has made us alive: "for good works." We don't obey (do good works) to condition God's love, but to the believer, "obedience (good works) is the sphere in which we enjoy God's love."[3] You have been made alive for a purpose: to image God by walking in the good works he has prepared for you. Walk in them for the glory of God and for the good of those around you.

---

3 Ligon Duncan, "The Whole in Our Holiness," sermon, *T4G.org*, https://t4g.org/resources/ligon-duncan/the-whole-in-our-holiness.

FAITH IN CHRIST

Day 2

READ: GALATIANS 2:20; EPHESIANS 3:16-17

I am an ardent proponent of catechisms, especially for teaching children. We use the Westminster Kids' Catechism[1] during family worship each evening in our home, and it is amazing to hear young children recite foundational Christian truths—I cannot recommend catechesis enough.

Not surprisingly, catechisms are also incredibly helpful for adults. They are designed to take biblical concepts and condense them into (relatively) short, memorable questions and answers to help you remember and retain them better.

---

1 Learn more about *The Kids' Catechism: An Introduction to the Shorter Catechism at The Westminster Standard*, https://thewestminsterstandard.org/The-Kids-Catechism/, accessed May 13, 2022.

I would like to begin today's devotional by considering two questions and answers from a catechism published by The Gospel Coalition and Crossway: *The New City Catechism.*

> **Question 29: How can we be saved?**
>
> **Answer:** Only by faith in Jesus Christ and in his substitutionary atoning death on the cross; so even though we are guilty of having disobeyed God and are still inclined to all evil, nevertheless, God, without any merit of our own but only by pure grace, imputes to us the perfect righteousness of Christ when we repent and believe in him.
>
> **Question 30: What is faith in Jesus Christ?**
>
> **Answer:** Faith in Jesus Christ is acknowledging the truth of everything that God has revealed in his Word, trusting in him, and also receiving and resting on him alone for salvation as he is offered in the gospel.[2]

When Paul and Silas were beaten and thrown into prison for proclaiming the truth of the gospel, God showed himself strong and rescued them in a miraculous way. When the jailer saw the power of God displayed, his eyes were opened to the reality of who he was before God. He fell down trembling before Paul and Silas, asking them an all-important question:

---

2 Published in partnership with The Gospel Coalition, *New City Catechism: 52 Questions and Answers for Our Hearts and Minds* (Wheaton, IL: Crossway, 2017), 74-77.

"What must I do to be saved?"[3]

Praise God we are not left without an answer to this question! Paul and Silas answered the jailer, "Believe in the Lord Jesus Christ, and you will be saved, you and your household" (Acts 16:31). In his 1828 *American Dictionary of the English Language*, Noah Webster (1758-1843) wrote, "To believe on, is to trust, to place full confidence in, to rest upon with faith."[4] Webster is far from being the first person to connect these two words: belief and faith are not the same, but they are inseparable. Ephesians 2:8 says we are saved "*by* grace...*through* faith" (emphasis mine). Our faith does not save us in and of itself, but we claim the promises of God and believe in Christ as he is offered to us in the gospel *through faith*—and *he* saves us. Faith, then, is necessary for salvation.

If faith in Christ is necessary for salvation, it is of utmost importance we understand what faith in Christ *is*. I referenced *The New City Catechism* earlier because I particularly like the way it defines faith in Christ as acknowledging, trusting, receiving, and resting. We've already discussed acknowledging "the truth of everything God has revealed in his Word" and "trusting in him" (like the Philippian jailer, we recognize that the only way we can be saved is to believe on Jesus Christ alone for salvation). But this is simply the beginning of our journey of faith. Faith is not

---

3 This event is recorded in Acts 16:25-34.

4 Noah Webster, *American Dictionary of the English Language*, First Edition (Chesapeake, VA: Foundation for American Christian Education, 1967), https://webstersdictionary1828.com/Dictionary/believe, accessed May 13, 2022.

a one-time event. The Christian life is a life of faith—every moment, every day. As stated in the outline, "We appropriate and continue to live out of this union [with Christ] through faith."

You read Galatians 2:20 at the very beginning of this devotional, which says, "I have been crucified with Christ. It is no longer I who live, but Christ who lives in me. And the life I now live in the flesh *I live by faith in the Son of God*, who loved me and gave himself for me" (emphasis mine). Paul was correcting theological error in the Galatian church and asked them, "Having begun in the Spirit, are you now being perfected by the flesh?" (Galatians 3:3). He's essentially saying, "You began this walk in faith—do you expect to continue in the power of the flesh?" Of course not. That's impossible. We live our daily lives—yes, even in these bodies of sinful flesh—by faith in the Son of God. Paul prayed for the Ephesian believers that God would strengthen them with power through his Spirit "so that Christ may dwell in [their] hearts through faith" (Ephesians 3:17).

Martin Luther said, "Faith is a living, daring confidence in God's grace, so sure and certain that a man would stake his life on it a thousand times."[5] I pray you have that kind of faith—that you wake up each day confident in the promises of God, knowing they cannot fail. Even when your faith is weak, he holds you fast—praise him!

---

5 Martin Luther, *Commentary on Romans*, translated by J. Theodore Mueller (Grand Rapids, MI: Kregel, 2003), xvii.

MEDITATE

If you have trusted in Christ as he is offered to you in the gospel, you have begun this journey in faith (Ephesians 2:8-9). Your union with Christ is also lived out, day by day, in faith. Has the life-giving message of the gospel grown stale to you? Pray and ask God to rejuvenate your faith and restore to you the joy of your salvation as you consider his work on your behalf this Holy Week.

CORAM DEO

The whole of the Christian life is a life of faith. But remember this: The assurance of who you are in Christ (and your standing before God) is not rooted in the strength of your faith. Our faith is fickle and weak and wavering. It is not the strength of your faith that saves you, but the object of your faith: Jesus Christ. Walk in confidence today, but put no confidence in yourself—rest in Jesus alone. He is your salvation.

JUSTIFIED IN CHRIST

Day 3

READ: 2 CORINTHIANS 5:21; PHILIPPIANS 3:8-9; ROMANS 3:23-25

In modern evangelicalism, the word "justification" seems to have fallen on hard times. As the modern church has distanced itself from biblical teachings on sin and our need to be made right before God, it makes sense that such a word would lose relevance. However, the importance of the doctrine of justification cannot be overstated.

The Bible uses justification and sanctification (more on that tomorrow) to express the redemptive work of Christ on behalf of people like you and me—sinners. You may have noticed that a couple of today's Scripture readings don't actually contain the words "justified" or "justification." This isn't for lack of use in the Scriptures; Paul uses the terms often in his letters to the churches at Rome and Galatia (as seen in Romans 3:23-25). That said, the doctrine of justification is seen clearly in these texts.

In 2 Corinthians 5:21, Paul explains what Christ did on our behalf which effected our justification: our sin was laid on Christ, and his righteousness was applied to us. We call that imputation: what was ours (sin) was accounted to Christ (as though it were his), and what was his (righteousness) was accounted to us (as though it were ours). The end result: we "become the righteousness of God," and are therefore declared righteous—though we are sinful beings. This is what it means to be justified.

I once learned an "A-B-C-D" acronym to help describe what justification means, and I found it quite helpful, so I'll use it here.

A Justification is an **ACT** of God. It is not meant to describe the way God inwardly renews and transforms us, but it is a legal term: a declaration of our pardon. In justification, God declares the sinner righteous, pardoning them of all their sins at the very moment of conversion.

B This presents a problem: How can a just God declare sinners righteous when they are truly guilty of sin? What is the **BASIS** of this shocking legal declaration? God justifies the sinner on the basis of the obedience of Christ—the obedience that led him to the cross where he laid down his life. Christ's perfect obedience fully satisfies God's demands for the payment of sin. The debt is paid in full, the slate is wiped clean, and we are declared righteous (Romans 5:18-19; Philippians 2:8). However, we are not justified by our own works. It is through Christ's work on our behalf alone that we are justified. Our sin was laid on Jesus—who knew no sin—and in turn, his righteousness was transferred to us. Our sins were imputed to Christ, and his righteousness was imputed to us. What a beautiful exchange!

C We are not justified by our works, but we are justified through faith alone when we **CONFESS** faith in Christ (Romans 10:9) and his work on our behalf. However, faith is simply a God-ordained instrument; it is not a "work" wrought by us. Faith is not something we "work up" from within ourselves. We don't "meet God halfway" when we exercise faith in Christ. Faith does not add to what Christ has done, but it receives the righteousness of Jesus offered to us in the gospel (Romans 4:4-5).

D Lastly, those who have received saving faith and have been justified will **DEMONSTRATE** the authenticity of that faith by producing fruit. According to James 2:14-26, it is possible to make a *profession* of saving faith without actually *possessing* saving faith. But we must be careful here not to put the cart before the horse: **we are not justified by our good works.** Rather, true faith in Christ will result in *evidence* of such faith. Paul reminds us in Ephesians 2:10 that one of the reasons we have been justified is so that we accomplish the good works God has prepared for us! If you are in Christ, your justification is complete. You cannot earn favor with God by performing good works, but if you have been justified, good works *will* follow—to the glory of God.

So how does this all fit together? In its most basic form, salvation can be described as regeneration, justification, sanctification, and glorification. This is sometimes called the "golden chain of redemption." Let's break those four words down:

1. God has made us alive in Christ (regeneration).
2. God has pardoned our sin, declaring us righteous (justification).
3. God is working in us to make us more like Christ (sanctification).
4. God will raise us to everlasting life in perfect, glorified bodies which will be totally free from the presence and effects of sin (glorification).

The gospel is simple enough to be grasped and understood by a child, but its underpinnings are enough to boggle our minds and cause us to stand in awe and wonder of God's glorious plan of redemption. We cannot be justified apart from faith in Christ. We cannot exercise faith in Christ when we are dead in our trespasses and sins. We need new life—we need to be regenerated. So God does the miraculous work of making us alive in Christ, granting us faith to believe in Christ, then, at the moment of belief, applies Christ's righteousness to us—laying our sin on Jesus—and declaring us righteous. But don't miss this: **none** of it works without Christ. If there is no sacrifice on our behalf, we are still dead in our sins and there is no hope of being justified before God. Everything hinges on Jesus.

MEDITATE

If you are reading this devotional in the order of Holy Week, tomorrow is Spy Wednesday, when Judas betrayed Jesus into the hands of evil men, setting in motion the arrest, trial, and crucifixion of Jesus. Jesus was not ignorant of the wicked schemes of Satan which had enticed Judas. Jesus knew what he was walking into when he entered Gethsemane, but he did it anyway. He walked *toward* his death. For you. For me. And that perfect, righteous obedience is now reckoned to us! When God looks at you and me, he sees the very righteousness of Christ. Praise him!

CORAM DEO

If you are in Christ, you have been removed from death row and have been granted a full pardon. You have been declared righteous before God. That, my friend, is true freedom. Christ has set you free—don't submit again to the yoke of slavery in which sin had you bound (Galatians 5:1). Christ bore that sin in his body on the cross, giving you his righteousness in its place. Live in that freedom today!

SANCTIFIED IN CHRIST

Day 4

READ: 1 CORINTHIANS 1:30; JOHN 15:4-5; 2 CORINTHIANS 5:17

Sanctification has become a bit of a touchy subject these days. It can make some people uncomfortable because it can be easily misunderstood as a way to earn favor with God through the faithful, obedient performance of good works. However, Scripture simply does not teach this. As we have already seen in this study, our standing before God (justification) is a work of grace from beginning to end—it does not depend on us *at all.* And yet, in his divine providence, God has ordained that sanctification be a part of our salvation, which Jesus purchased with his own blood (1 Peter 1:17-19).[1]

1 While it is common in evangelical circles to use salvation and justification interchangeably, it is important to note that when I say "salvation" here, I mean God's redemptive work of salvation from beginning to end, not merely justification.

The Westminster Shorter Catechism defines sanctification as "the work of God's free grace, whereby we are renewed in the whole man after the image of God, and are enabled more and more to die unto sin, and live unto righteousness."[2] In other words, sanctification is a consistent, continuous process worked in each and every believer by God to make us look more like Jesus. By his Word and Spirit, God transforms us from "one degree of glory to another" (2 Corinthians 3:18). It is not an immediate eradication of sin, but it is more than the mere appearance of change. Sanctification is *real* transformation; it is the process of becoming more like our Savior, Jesus Christ.

As we are made more like Christ, we *look* more like Christ. Jesus said when we shine our light before others—which he equates to "good works" (cf. Ephesians 2:10)—others will see our good works and give glory to our Father. What's happening there? If we are performing good works in the presence of others, won't they be seeing *us?* As we saw yesterday, good works are quite useless as a means to earning God's grace; it simply cannot be done. How then do good works point others to the Father? In one of our passages for today, Paul writes, "And because of [God] you are in Christ Jesus, who became to us wisdom from God, righteousness and sanctification and redemption" (1 Corinthians 1:30). Follow the grammar here and consider what Paul is saying: "Christ... became...to us...sanctification." Our sanctification is not something we

---

2 Westminster Shorter Catechism (question 35), *The Westminster Standard*, https://thewestminsterstandard.org/Westminster-Shorter-Catechism/.

are required to "work up" within ourselves now that we are justified in Christ. Rather, we are given Christ, who *is* our sanctification! This is what it means to be sanctified in Christ: we are sanctified to God *through* our union with Christ.

If Christ has purchased our sanctification with his own blood, and he is himself our sanctification, this is not something we should take lightly. In fact, it's not optional: Peter instructs us in 1 Peter 1:15, "but as he who called you is holy, you also be holy in all your conduct." We are commanded to be holy in all our conduct. In other words, "Be like Jesus *in everything you do.*"

If that sounds overwhelming or even impossible, that's because it is—on your own. We have no hope for success in this area of the Christian life apart from the Word and Spirit of God. But don't be fooled into thinking there is some "secret sauce" to unlocking sanctification. God ordained that his work of salvation would be brought about by ordinary means, and your sanctification is no different. It's all of grace, and it's all Jesus—but it doesn't come about by kicking back and putting our feet up. God doesn't simply sprinkle us with sanctifying powder and magically sanctify us. We don't undergo a one-time grand gesture of outward transformation and consider our sanctification complete. It's a consistent, gradual process brought about by God through ordinary means. Pastor and author H. B. Charles Jr. said it this way: "It is the will of God to have the Spirit of God to use the word of God to make the children of God look like the Son of God."[3] Don't underestimate the power of the Word of God in your life—it is your life. It may sometimes feel like just reading a book, but rest assured: When you read God's Word, the Holy Spirit performs a miracle in the life of the believer. The Bible is living and active (Hebrews 4:12), and it feeds you, sustains you, and keeps your eyes fixed on Christ.

Your sanctification is every bit a work of God as your justification. God uses his Word and Spirit to conform you into the image of his Son (Romans 8:29). We cannot meditate on or appreciate our union with Christ—who loved us and gave himself for us (Galatians 2:20)—without considering sanctification. Thank God for this great gift of grace!

MEDITATE

Do you struggle with feeling like you're not any more like Jesus than you were a year ago? Meditate on today's Scripture readings and pray them as prayers of thanksgiving to God. Ask him to give you faith to trust wholly in Jesus. If you are in Christ, God is forming Christ in you (Galatians 4:19), and he *will* complete the work he started (Philippians 1:6). Every day, through the ups and downs, he is molding and transforming you to be conformed to the image of Christ.

---

3 H. B. Charles Jr. (@hbcharlesjr), Twitter post, June 24 ,2014, https://twitter.com/hbcharlesjr/status/481399088681091073, accessed May 13, 2022.

CORAM DEO

The fruit of justification is sanctification—and ultimately, glorification. If you are in Christ, you have been freed from the penalty of sin (justification) and the power of sin (sanctification), and one day, you will be free from the presence of sin (glorification). Christ's conquering of sin on the cross (it no longer has dominion over you!) means you can kill it. When you are tempted to sin, remember Christ. To live *coram deo* is to kill the sin he died to conquer. Walk as a child of light.

PERSEVERING IN CHRIST

Day 5

READ: JOHN 10:27-29; ROMANS 8:38-39; JUDE 24-25

One of the most precious promises from God is his promise to *keep* us. When Jesus says that he came to give his sheep eternal life (John 10:28), we can trust and believe that he means what he says. The life we have in Christ is truly eternal and unending. No one—not you, not anyone else—can snatch you out of his hand. As the song goes, "No power of hell, no scheme of man can ever pluck me from his hand!"[1] Nothing can separate us from the love of God in Christ Jesus.

We eagerly await the day when we will be raised in glorified bodies; when God will once again dwell with us. Until then, we are called to be

1 Keith and Kristyn Getty, "In Christ Alone," track 6 on *In Christ Alone*, Getty Music Label, compact disc.

faithful; to endure to the end (Matthew 10:22). If you're anything like me, a call to persevere (or endure) to the end is a bit overwhelming to hear. I have a strong desire to persevere in unwavering faith until my dying breath, but my flesh is so weak—I fail over and over again. Sometimes my faith is fickle and wavering. Sometimes I doubt the promises of God. How could someone like me even hope to endure to the end? The tenth chapter of the Gospel of John is the comforting and glorious promise to which I cling for dear life. Jesus says he gives his sheep "eternal life, and they will never perish, and no one will snatch them out of [his] hand" (John 10:28).

So why do we fear? If we could take hold of this truth down deep in our bones, we would experience overwhelming freedom and joy—we would have no reason to worry! And yet, we do. Why? The answer is painfully simple: our sin. We are saved forever, never to be utterly lost again, but we live in bodies of sinful flesh. Our physical bodies and our sinful nature war against the Spirit's work in our lives, and when we give into temptation, we are carried away into sin. When we sin, we grieve the Holy Spirit within us (Ephesians 4:30), wound our conscience, and "sometimes for a while lose the sense of God's favor."[2] We don't actually lose God's favor—that cannot be earned or lost by any actions of our own. But when we sin against God, we certainly lose a sense of his favor. We feel separated from him again. He feels distant, dark, and cold.

---

2 Canons of Dort, "Fifth Head of Doctrine: The Perseverance of the Saints," Article 5, https://www.williamburrows2.com/Canons-of-Dort/. Public Domain.

But these are nothing more than lies of the enemy. God leads us with fatherly affection to repentance by his kindness (Romans 2:4).

Because our salvation is rooted and grounded in Christ and is secured on the basis of his work on our behalf (see "Introduction"), it cannot be lost. God does not take back his gracious gift of salvation, even in our greatest sins. If you belong to him—if you are his sheep—he will *never* let you wander so far as to lose your standing before him or a place in his family. We were born again of an incorruptible and imperishable seed (1 Peter 1:23); our adoption cannot and will not ever be revoked. We belong—body and soul, in life and in death—to our faithful Savior, Jesus Christ.[3]

However, we must be careful not to be glib or careless with our doctrine of perseverance. Those who endure to the end will be saved—that is true. God is the one bearing up his sheep, keeping them from falling and causing them to endure to the end—that is also true. But this is intimately connected with yesterday's topic: sanctification. God preserves his children through the ongoing work of the Holy Spirit in our lives. That is, through his Word and Spirit, God keeps us from falling away completely. But it also means that when we stumble, we are met with the kindness of God—not to tell us "it's okay," but to call us to confess and repent of our sin. He inflicts us with godly sorrows meant to lead us away from sin and death and into a restored relationship with

---

3 Heidelberg Catechism, Question 1, https://www.williamburrows2.com/Heidelberg-Catechism/, accessed May 13, 2022. Public Domain.

him. He may do this through a friend or family member who lovingly calls out your sin, through a pastor who faithfully preaches the Word to you, or through your own reading of the Bible. God would rather take your right hand than for you to be utterly lost (Matthew 5:30).

The author of Hebrews exhorts us:"Therefore, since we are surrounded by so great a cloud of witnesses, let us also lay aside every weight, and sin which clings so closely, and let us run with endurance the race that is set before us, looking to Jesus, the founder and perfecter of our faith" (Hebrews 12:1-2). He has just gone through an incredible history of Old Testament saints who believed and claimed the promises of God, though they died without ever seeing those promises fulfilled. Those faith-filled saints are now watching us run our race, and the writer of Hebrews uses them as an example to encourage us if we should stumble. But just a few verses later, he quotes a passage from Proverbs as a gentle and loving warning: "My son, do not regard lightly the discipline of the Lord, nor be weary when reproved by him. For the Lord disciplines the one he loves, and chastises every son whom he receives" (Hebrews 12:5-6, cited from Proverbs 3:11-12).

This discipline is unpleasant and painful (Hebrews 12:11), but it stands as proof of John 10:27-29 and Jude 24-25. Our Good Shepherd isn't going to simply let his sheep wander back into the darkness of the world. He calls us to confess our sins, reminding us that when we do, "he is faithful and just to forgive us our sins and to cleanse us from all unrighteousness" (1 John 1:9). Those who persevere to the end are not exempt from temptation and sin. They do not achieve some sort of elevated Christianity where they no longer sin. But they do *repent* more. As we grow in faith, we become better "repenters." We don't want the discipline or the sense of losing God's favor—we love and cherish his presence. We deeply desire to commune with him with no sin standing in the way.

Before we conclude, there is a strong warning we need to heed in the text of Hebrews 12. If the Lord indeed disciplines his own, we will not enjoy sin. Of course, sin is pleasurable for a season (Hebrews 11:25), but no son or daughter of God can endure the broken fellowship sin brings. Those who belong to God will return in repentance contrition. We are told in 1 John, "No one who abides in him keeps on sinning; no one who keeps on sinning has either known him or seen him...No one born of God makes a practice of sinning, for God's seed abides in him; and he cannot keep on sinning, because he has been born of God" (1 John 3:6, 9). These are some unsettling words, but they are written for our reproof, correction, and training in righteousness (2 Timothy 3:16). If God disciplines his own, and we are able to sin without discipline, we would do well to heed Paul's admonition: "Examine yourselves, to see whether you are in the faith" (2 Corinthians 13:5).

God's promise of preservation does not extend beyond the sheepfold. He keeps his own, and he disciplines them when they stray into sin. When you experience the conviction of the Holy Spirit in your sin, thank the Lord. It's not pleasant at the time, but it is a wonderful reminder of his loving kindness and grace which leads you to repentance and restored communion with him. If you belong to him, persevere in faith, knowing it is he who holds you—and he cannot fail. If you don't yet belong to him, he invites you in with open arms. Jesus' sheep hear his voice—and they come when they are called. If he is calling you, run to him! He is waiting with open arms to shelter you safely in his arms.

MEDITATE

The doctrine of the perseverance of the saints should never lead us to become proud or slothful in our walk with Christ. It's all Christ from beginning to end. If any part of it depended on us, we would fail and fall away. This doctrine should cause us to humble ourselves before God and make us more fervent in our prayers as we work out our own salvation with fear and trembling (Philippians 2:12). However, we ought not cripple ourselves with fear. Take hold of God's promises to hold you fast.

CORAM DEO

Those who have been redeemed do not persevere to the end not by any merit or strength of their own, but because "the eternal God is [their] refuge, and underneath are the everlasting arms" (Deuteronomy 33:27). The Christian life cannot be lived apart from Christ. Each time you feel the loving discipline of God when you sin, breathe a prayer of gratitude for his fatherly affection and kindness that leads you to repentance. Trust his promises to preserve your faith. He is God almighty. Walk before him and be blameless (Genesis 17:1).

CRUCIFIED WITH CHRIST

Day 6

READ: GALATIANS 2:20; GALATIANS 5:24; ROMANS 6:6-14

If you began reading this devotional on Palm Sunday, you will likely read this entry on Good Friday. It seems fitting to meditate on being crucified with Christ today. The cross of Christ is a great mystery; the worst thing that has ever happened in the world and the best thing that has ever happened in the world. We break promises, so God keeps his. We run from God, so he runs to us. We suffer for sin, so the Savior suffers for us. Our story is the story of God doing what we can't, in order to make up for us doing what we shouldn't. The Christ suffers for our sins, that we might share in his sinlessness.[1]

1 Most of this paragraph is cited from Kevin DeYoung, *The Biggest Story: How the Snake Crusher Brings Us Back to the Garden* (Wheaton, IL: Crossway, 2015), 106-107.

How can sinful people—even redeemed sinners—share in Christ's sinlessness? Before we get too far, I want to first make this clear: we will never be sinless this side of heaven. There are some who teach this, but it is a doctrine not found in the Scriptures. It's a myth. We are chosen, redeemed children of God, but we dwell in earthen vessels (2 Corinthians 4:7 KJV). We will never be free from the presence of sin until we are with Christ in our eternal home. But we are *redeemed.* In other words, Christ has purchased our freedom by dying in our place. We are restored to fellowship and union with God because of the sacrifice of Jesus. We have been set free from the bondage of sin. Sin no longer has dominion over us! How then are we to reconcile being free from sin if we still sin?

Martin Luther coined the Latin phrase "Simul Justus et Peccator." In English, it means that if you are in Christ, you are "at the same time just (righteous) and a sinner." You are declared righteous, though you are still quite capable of sinning. Again, this is a great mystery. Paul said in 2 Corinthians 5:17 that to be in Christ is to be "a new creation. The old has passed away; behold, the new has come." So we are a new creation—we have a new nature! When Paul says "the old has passed away," he speaks of the "old man," the once-enslaved-to-sin person you were before you met Jesus. According to Romans 6:6, our old self was crucified with Christ—we're no longer enslaved!

One might think that because the old self has been crucified with Christ, we need not worry about sin. It is true that sin no longer has dominion over us—it can never "own" us again. But we have not yet received our glorified bodies. So how are we to live as a new creation in Christ? Paul continues in Romans: "you...must consider yourselves dead to sin and alive to God in Christ Jesus. Let not sin therefore reign in your mortal body, to make you obey its passions" (Romans 6:11-12). On the heels of this glorious declaration of our "old self" being crucified with Christ, Paul turns around and says "so don't let sin reign over you." Remember, Paul is speaking under the divine inspiration of the Holy Spirit of God. He didn't make a mistake here. He's not confused. He knows that our hearts are "desperately wicked" (Jeremiah 17:9 KJV). Paul knows the very sin which caused the hearts of the Israelite children to turn away from God and long to become enslaved in Egypt again would seek to lure us away, too.

Our sinful nature hates our new nature. It wants to overcome it. It wants to take you back to where you were before Christ found you—back to when you were sin's slave. But what does Paul point to as our basis of freedom from sin? Christ's crucifixion. We have died with Christ! Our sin has been nailed to the cross, washed in his blood. Past, present, future—it's all been paid for! The sins we practice in secret, the sins the enemy would use to shame us before the Father, and the sins which so easily entangle us have been covered with the blood of Christ—all of them. The gossip you engage in at work, the sexual sins you try to hide from your friends and family, the bitterness and anger your harbor toward others—forgiven completely, without exception.

Today, when you remember Christ crucified, remember this: He was crucified for you. Not in a general sense, but in a personal sense. He died for the sins you committed yesterday. And the day before. And last year. Jesus died for you. And when he died, he took your sin upon his shoulders—nailing it to the cross—so you could be free from its power. Do you feel helpless in your battle with sin? Look to the cross. Remind the enemy why we call today "Good" Friday. Remind him that he no longer has dominion over you—you are free!

MEDITATE

With his dying breath, Jesus brought you everlasting life. His sacrifice broke the curse of sin which once enslaved you—you are free! Spend some time in prayer as you meditate on today's Scripture. If you have grown cold or apathetic to the glorious message of the gospel, ask God to increase your faith and give you a fresh look at the cross. Christ has died for *you*.

CORAM DEO

The crucified life is a life of selflessness. We once were dead, but we now live—through Christ who lives in us. Though you still live in a fleshly body, live by faith in the Son of God who loves you and gave himself for you.

RAISED WITH CHRIST

Day 7

READ: COLOSSIANS 3:1-4; 1 CORINTHIANS 15:22

In his letter to the Corinthians, Paul wrote, "if Christ has not been raised, then all our preaching is useless, and your faith is useless...if Christ has not been raised, your faith is futile, and you are still in your sins" (1 Corinthians 15:14, 17). Jesus fulfilled every prophecy he was meant to fulfill. He was from the right city, from the right family, and did the right things. He was meek, humble, and compassionate. He performed miracles, healed the sick and raised the dead.

And yet, Paul says with confidence that if Christ had not been raised, our faith is futile and we are still in our sins. This is strong language; what he's really saying is that if Christ had not been raised, then Christ's death would be worthless. It's a heavy thing to say, it's a heavy thing to hear, and it's a heavy thing to ponder. Paul finished this thought by saying, "If in this life only we have hope in Christ, we are of all men most miserable" (1 Corinthians 15:19 KJV). If our hope in Christ dies with our mortal bodies, this broken world is as good as it's going to get for us. For us to truly grasp the wonder of the resurrection, we must ponder this weighty thought.

In Ephesians 2 (my second favorite chapter in the entire Bible), Paul paints a dark picture of our lives before Christ. Dead in our sins, slaves to self and Satan, living under the wrath of God. Then, he says, "But God..." It's hard to read those two simple words without being moved. Many times, those two words have brought tears to my eyes. *But God.* Because God is rich in mercy and has great love for us, our lives are forever changed. We are made alive in Christ!

Paul employs this same effective, joy-inducing conjunction here in 1 Corinthians 15. If Christ has not been raised, everything we've believed and everything we've been doing and preaching is worthless. We're still in our sins, and of all men on earth, we are the most miserable. BUT... here's the shift: "But in fact Christ *has* been raised from the dead, the firstfruits of those who have fallen asleep. For as by a man came death, by a man has come also the resurrection of the dead" (1 Corinthians 15:20-21, emphasis mine). Christ's resurrection is our promise; the sign of our sure hope that we WILL be raised to life everlasting. In verse 22, Paul said, "Just as everyone dies because we all belong to Adam, everyone who belongs to Christ will be given new life" (1 Corinthians

15:22 NLT). This is good news—the best news, in fact. Our faith is not in vain. We are not still in our sins. Christ's death was *not* useless. We will be raised.

So, what about now? Does this matter for our lives today? Absolutely. This is an example of the "already and not yet" tension we live in. We *will* be raised; that's the "not yet." But we *have been* raised (Colossians 3:1); that's the "already." This is not a mistake or typo in the Scriptures. It's a dual reality. We have been raised and we will be raised. We are saved (Ephesians 2:8-9), we are being saved (1 Corinthians 1:18; 2 Corinthians 2:15), and we will be saved (Romans 5:9). All three of these tenses are used in Scripture in relation to our salvation, which is directly tied to the resurrection. So what does it mean to be raised with Christ now? Let's look at three implications of the resurrection:

1. We have died with Christ.

We looked at what it means to be crucified with Christ yesterday, but Paul tells us in Colossians 3:3 that being raised with Christ reminds us that we have died with Christ. To die with Christ means we are dead to sin. As Horatio Spafford said in his famous hymn, "It Is Well," our sin is "nailed to the cross" and we "bear it no more." Praise the Lord! Sin no longer has dominion over you (Romans 6:1-14). Being raised with Christ means we are freed from sin, *because* we have died with Christ.

2. Our life is hidden with Christ.

When Adam and Eve sinned in the Garden of Eden, their first instinct was to hide themselves from God. Their eyes were opened to the reality of their sin, and they feared God in a way they never had before. In the book of Revelation, we see a similar scene when Jesus comes in judgment and wrath. Those who have rejected and blasphemed Christ are now terrified when God's mercy is removed from the earth. Revelation 6:15-16 says they will call on mountains and rocks to fall on them to hide them "from the face of him who is seated on the throne, and from the wrath of the Lamb." Between these two bookends (Genesis and Revelation) we have the message of the gospel: the preaching of the cross of Jesus. We come to Christ clothed in our shame and filthy rags, and he gives us his righteousness. He becomes our cleft in the rock—our hiding place. To be raised with Christ is to be hidden in Christ; we are saved from the wrath to come.

3. We will appear with Christ in Glory.

Paul finishes these few verses by reminding us of the coming glory of an eternity with Christ and God our Father. Try as we might, we simply cannot fathom nor explain what awaits us in glory. But we know this: our God will once again dwell with us, and we will know him as we are known (1 Corinthians 13:12). Christ, who is our life, will one day return. And when he does, we will be joined to him in a way we cannot now comprehend: in glorified bodies, without the presence or stain of sin, seeing God face-to-face. This is our blessed hope (Titus 2:13). Being raised with Christ means he will come back for those for whom he died, and "so shall we ever be with the Lord" (1 Thessalonians 4:17 KJV).

MEDITATE

Do you believe Christ really rose from the dead? Paul stakes everything on the resurrection. If Jesus hasn't been raised, there is no forgiveness of sin. His perfect life of obedience and his sacrificial death are rendered worthless if there is no resurrection. "The resurrection is God's 'Amen' to Jesus' loud cry: 'It is finished,' and therefore the guarantee that by Jesus' death the believer has indeed been reconciled to God."[1] Consider the implications of the resurrection of Christ and how it is connected to his promise to raise you up with Christ on the last day.

CORAM DEO

Living in light of the resurrection takes gospel focus. We have experienced a type of resurrection in Christ: being made alive in him through his work of redemption on our behalf. But we await our full resurrection—being raised at the last day to begin lives of eternity with Jesus. Surely that promise encourages us to walk with him *now!* We don't have to wait until heaven to live joy-filled, grace-empowered lives. You are a new creation. The old has died. The new has come. The perfect will come.

---

1 J. A. Schep, "Resurrection of Jesus Christ," *Zondervan Pictorial Bible Encyclopedia, Vol. V* (Grand Rapids, MI: Zondervan, 1975), 83.

GLORIFIED WITH CHRIST

Day 8

READ: COLOSSIANS 3:4; 1 THESSALONIANS 4:16-17; ROMANS 8:30

Holy Week began with Palm Sunday, when we remember Jesus' triumphal entry into Jerusalem. To many of the Jews, this moment was their moment of glory; the long-awaited time had come. Jesus is now entering the city, and soon he will tear off his robe, revealing his armor and sword and lead them into a bloody, victorious overthrow of the Romans! But this was not at all what Jesus was preparing to do. In fact, he was preparing to do just the opposite. Rather than overthrowing the powers that be, he would offer his life up to them. God the Father, at this very moment, was setting the plan in motion to deliver Jesus up "according to the definite plan and foreknowledge of God" to be "crucified and killed by the hands of lawless men" (Acts 2:23).

A few days later, during his longest recorded prayer in Scripture, Jesus prayed, "Father, the hour has come; glorify your Son that the Son may glorify you....I glorified you on earth, having accomplished the work that you gave me to do. And now, Father, glorify me in your own presence with the glory that I had with you before the world existed" (John 17:1, 4-5). Towards the end of that prayer, Jesus prays this: "The glory that you have given me I have given to them, that they may be one even as we are one, I in them and you in me" (John 17:22-23).[1]

King Jesus does not wield his kingship for selfish gain or to protect himself from what is to come. He willingly lays down his life for his sheep. Why? He longs to glorify the Father. As he glorifies the Father, the Father glorifies him—and in turn, Jesus gives that glory to us! We share in his glory. Romans 8:29-30 says, "For those whom he foreknew he also predestined to be conformed to the image of his Son, in order that he might be the firstborn among many brothers. And those whom he predestined he also called, and those whom he called he also justified, and those whom he justified he also glorified."

Jesus willingly gave himself for us, but he did not cease being our king in doing so. Three days after Jesus laid down his life, God raised him from the dead into a glorified body which will never taste of death again. To be glorified is to be restored to perfection. If God had not raised Jesus from the dead, his body would have decomposed just as any other

1 This prayer is known as the "High Priestly Prayer," and it takes up the entire chapter of John 17.

human body would have. Jesus subjected himself to a literal human body, capable of being wounded and killed. But God raised Jesus into a body which would never be wounded or killed again. Perfect restoration. And those who are in Christ have been glorified in him.

It is true that we dwell in bodies of sinful flesh, but our glorification is secured in Christ's glorification—it is as good as done! Just as Christ lives to never die again, so shall we. We will one day be glorified, our bodies being fully restored to their rightful place in God's new heaven and new earth, where there is no pain, no tears, and no death.

Some call Romans 8:29-30 the "golden chain of salvation" because each link in the chain cannot be broken from the rest. Those who are foreknown will be predestined. Those who are predestined will be called. Those who are called will be justified. And those who are justified will be glorified. In other words, God's holy work of salvation cannot not be interrupted or thwarted. When God begins the work of salvation, rest assured it will be carried out to completion. Paul says in Philippians 1:6, "I am sure of this, that he who began a good work in you will bring it to completion at the day of Jesus Christ." The chain cannot be broken. King Jesus cannot be dethroned. His glory cannot be diminished. We will be glorified in Christ and share in his rule and reign.

As you face the new week, rejoice in Jesus as your King and joyfully anticipate that wonderful day when Jesus will "transform [your] lowly body to be like his glorious body" (Philippians 3:21), and "so shall we ever be with the Lord" (1 Thessalonians 4:17 KJV). The chronic pain which seems to plague your every waking moment, the addiction you can't seem to break free from, the anxiety that keeps you awake all night—it will all be made right. To be glorified is to be free from every stain and curse of sin. Not a trace will remain!

MEDITATE

Suggested prayer: "Jesus, there's no one like you. You—the only King who can make every other king bow down in awe and reverence before your throne—became like us to redeem us and reconcile us back to the Father. You glorified the Father in everything you did, and he glorified you. Jesus, I worship you as my King, and I long for the day I will stand in your presence, glorified. Now, I see through a glass dimly; but then, I will see you face to face. What a day that will be! Until then, hold me fast. Remind me daily that I am not my own, but belong—body and soul, in life and in death—to you, my faithful Savior, Jesus Christ. Amen."

CORAM DEO

Paul writes in Romans 8:18, "For I consider that the sufferings of this present time are not worth comparing with the glory that is to be revealed to us." The difference between the trials and suffering we experience and the glory that awaits the child of God is so vastly different we can't really even comprehend it. There is no comparison at all. But we can be assured of this: when pain, sorrow, or troubles of any kind threaten to discourage us, know that the glory that is to come will make it all worth it. Comfort one another with these words.

SCRIPTURE INDEX

EXPLORE HOSANNA REVIVAL PUBLISHING

Hosanna Revival Publishing was launched in August 2020 as a way to provide our community with rich Bible study and devotional content written by our community. Our mission has always been to excite people about engaging with Scripture by creating beautiful and intentional tools for their lives, and Hosanna Revival Publishing does exactly that. We work side by side with authors and aspiring authors from our community to create beautiful devotionals and Bible studies to help people engage more deeply with Jesus and his Word.

Choose your devotional from our featured library by scanning the QR code to the right.

PRAY LIKE THIS
Katie Noble

I AM NOT IN CHARGE
Ness Cannon

SONGS FOR THE SUFFERING
Julia Allspaw

YET
Erica Boden

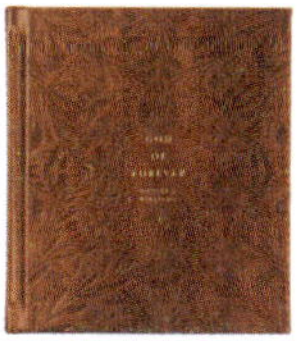

GOD OF FOREVER
Haylee Williams

ROOTED TO RISE
Haley Crabtree

THE STORY CIRCLE
Joshua Lenon

BEAUTY NOT BEHELD
Paige Stitt McBride

USE CODE FREE5

to get $5 off your devotional

** Offer valid for a limited time only. **

ABOUT THE AUTHOR

Will Burrows is the director of publishing and executive editor of Hosanna Revival and serves as the director of worship at Christian Reformed Church of Saint Joseph, Michigan. He has served in various positions of music and pastoral ministry for more than ten years and has assisted in church planting. Will and his wife, Alicia, have five sons and live on Michigan's west coast with their beautiful Australian shepherd, Clover.